MW01231614

YOUNG PROFILES

Hanson

Paul Joseph
ABDO Publishing Company

visit us at
www.abdopub.com

Published by ABDO Publishing Company 4940 Viking Drive, Edina, Minnesota 55435.
Copyright © 1999 by Abdo Consulting Group, Inc. International copyrights reserved in all countries. No part of this book may be reproduced in any form without written permission from the publisher.

Printed in the United States.

Photo credits: AP/Wide World; Shooting Star
Edited by Tamara L. Britton
Contributing editor A.T. McKenna

To my niece Gracie (Hanson's #1 fan)

Library of Congress Cataloging-in-Publication Data

Joseph, Paul, 1970-
    Hanson / Paul Joseph.
    p. cm. -- (Young profiles)
    Includes index.
    Summary: Describes the path that three young brothers took from hometown musicians in Tulsa, Oklahoma, to the release of their hit single "MMMBop."
    ISBN 1-57765-321-1 (hardcover)
    ISBN 1-57765-333-5 (paperback)
    1. Hanson (Musical group--Juvenile literature. 2. Rock musicians--United States--Biography--Juvenile literature. 3. Rock groups--United States--Juvenile literature. [1. Hanson (Musical group) 2. Musicians. 3. Rock groups.] I. Title. II. Series.
    ML3930.H28J6 2000
    782.42166'092'2--dc21
    [B]
                                                     98-40005
                                                     CIP
                                                        AC

Contents

MMMBop to the Top 4

Profile of Hanson 6

Middle of Nowhere 8

Singing in the Beginning 10

Far, Far Away 12

Back to Tulsa 14

The Hanson Brothers 16

Taking Aim 18

Boomerang 20

Another Album 22

The Real Deal 24

The Sky's the Limit 26

Secrets about Hanson 28

The Final Words From Hanson 29

Glossary 30

Hanson on the Web 31

Index 32

MMMBop
to the Top

Isaac, Taylor, and Zachary Hanson are the talented and cute brothers who took the music world completely by surprise in 1997.

The three brothers from Tulsa, Oklahoma, who named their band Hanson, were not prepared for the success of the hit song "MMMBop." Mercury Records released the song on March 24, 1997, to radio stations—but not stores. Around the entire country people were going crazy for the song.

In early May, the single was sold in stores and by the end of the month it was the number one song in the country. In its first week in stores it sold 140,000 copies! Most radio stations played it more than 50 times a week!

"MMMBop" wasn't just a hit in the United States but also was number one in Canada, England, Germany, France,

Australia, and Japan. The video received major air play, too.

Many believed that Hanson would have their 15 minutes of fame and fade away quietly. But Hanson is more than a flash in the pan teeny-bop band. They are the real deal. Each brother plays his own instruments and writes music and **lyrics**. They can **harmonize** together with ease. The unbelievable part is that the three brothers are just barely teenagers!

Although "MMMBop" was a surprise hit, the brothers worked many long years to make it. They were not put together by a music company, but rather by themselves. Hanson had many **rejections**, but after five years they took "MMMBop" to the top and they are determined to stay there.

Isaac, Zachary, and Taylor Hanson

Profile of Hanson

Isaac

Full Name: Clarke Isaac Hanson

Nickname: Ike

Birthday: November 17, 1980

Height: 5 feet, 8 inches

Instrument: Guitar

Favorite Musician: Alanis Morissette

Favorite Sports: Hockey, in-line skating

Favorite Color: Green

Favorite Food: Pizza, mashed potatoes

Taylor

Full Name: Jordan Taylor Hanson

Nickname: Tay

Birthday: March 14, 1983

Height: 5 feet, 6 inches

Instrument: Keyboard, synthesizer, and bongos

Favorite Musicians: Counting Crows, Spin Doctors, Natalie Merchant

Favorite Sports: Soccer, basketball, in-line skating

Favorite Color: Red

Favorite Food: Pizza, McDonald's

Zachary

Full Name: Zachary Walker Hanson

Nickname: Zac

Birthday: October 22, 1985

Height: 5 feet, 3 inches

Instrument: Drums

Favorite Musicians: Aerosmith

Favorite Sports: In-line skating, basketball

Favorite Color: Blue

Favorite Food: Pizza

Middle of Nowhere

Hanson's smash debut **album** *Middle of Nowhere,* was named in honor of their hometown. The Hanson story begins in Tulsa, Oklahoma, which most people think of as middle America. Tulsa is the second largest city in Oklahoma. It's a laid back city where people are friendly and the hottest music isn't Hanson, it's country and western.

Ike, Tay, and Zac are very much a product of their mid-America hometown. The Hanson family has long roots in Tulsa. The boys' parents, Walker and Diana, were born there. Grandparents, uncles, aunts, and cousins live there, too.

The brothers got their musical talent from their parents. Walker and Diana both loved music. Diana majored in music in college. Walker was an excellent guitarist and singer. The two joined a gospel musical group called the Horizons. The Horizons traveled the country performing in churches.

After getting married, Walker and Diana wanted to start a family. They gave up on music and bought a small house in their hometown. Walker took a job as an **accountant** for an oil drilling company.

On November 17, 1980, the couple's first child was born. The baby boy was named Clarke Isaac (Ike). On March 14, 1983, the second son arrived. This one was named Jordan Taylor (Tay). On October 22, 1985, the family was blessed with their third boy in a row, Zachary Walker (Zac). No one knew then, but the band Hanson had been born.

The Hanson brothers grew up in Tulsa, Oklahoma.

Singing in the Beginning

As youngsters, the boys remembered two things: the music around them and the closeness they shared. Their parents always played music in the house. Much of the music was gospel, but other types of music were played too, including rock-n-roll, R&B, and classical.

The brothers learned to **harmonize** and had wonderful voices. All three loved to sing together. Making music became their primary "play" activity. Their parents never made them sing or even asked them to sing, the boys just did it on their own.

Ike, Tay, and Zac rarely watched television or played video games. Their hobbies were playing sports, biking, and in-line skating. But above everything, it was their music. The three young boys began **composing** their own songs.

Soon Ike, Tay, and Zac were getting to be very good at writing and singing. Their three-part harmonies were supertight, and soon they had almost an **album** full of original songs. Although the songs were not the greatest, the three had a lot of talent. To top it off, they were not even 10 years old!

Just getting started, (L to R) Zac, Tay, and Ike.

Far, Far Away

In 1988, Walker Hanson, who was now the director of international accounting for his company, was transferred out of the country for his job. This meant that the entire family had to move away from Tulsa.

The Hanson family spent the next year in Ecuador, Venezuela, Trinidad, and Tobago. Their schooling did not change. The Hanson boys were home-schooled. This meant that they did not go to traditional school, but had school at home and their mother was their teacher.

As they prepared for their big move, the Hanson brothers were worried about their music. Because of the language and **cultural** differences, the brothers knew that they would not be able to hear their favorite music on the radio—in fact there was no radio! So the family brought along a whole bunch of different tapes to listen to.

Living out of the country really brought the family together and the boys worked even more on their music. Every day they would sing and write and at night their parents would join in and sing too.

Life away from the United States had its difficulties. There was no television or radio, there were also no cars, malls, or fast food. But the year away was great. They met many different people and saw wild parrots, crocodiles, and iguanas. They had lots of freedom, became closer as a family, and got to work on their music.

Hanson at the MTV Movie Awards, 1997.

Back to Tulsa

In 1989, the Hanson family moved back to Tulsa. Ike, Tay, and Zac now had a little sister named Jessica who was born in 1988. In 1991, another little sister would join the family, named Avery. Brother Mac came along in 1994. The newest Hanson, daughter Zoe, joined the family in 1998.

Ike, Tay, and Zac continued working on their music. At first the brothers didn't write down their music, they would just play it off the top of their heads. Then in 1990, Ike wrote down the music and **lyrics** to "Rain Falling Down." It was their first official song.

All three boys began taking piano lessons at a young age. All three were excellent players. However, Tay was the best and picked it up the quickest. In spite of all their musical talent, the work they put in, and the encouragement from their parents, Ike, Tay, and Zac never thought about playing outside of the home.

At the end of 1991, at their father's company Christmas party, everything changed. All of the company's employees and their families were invited to the party. For some reason Ike, Tay, and Zac, all of eleven, eight, and six years old, got up and started to perform. With no instruments, the boys just lined up, snapped their fingers, and began harmonizing on a few rock-n-roll oldies.

The **audience** was amazed at the youngsters. After they were finished, the crowd went wild and asked for more songs. After that performance the three brothers knew that they wanted to become professional singers.

Isaac, Zac, and Taylor Hanson perform "MmmBop" during a free concert at the City Center Mall in Columbus, Ohio.

The Hanson Brothers

In 1992, Ike, Tay, and Zac started their own music group. They called their group the Hanson Brothers and began working on their act. Since the boys could only play piano, they stuck with what they knew best—singing.

The Hanson Brothers would perform *a cappella* versions of their favorite songs. The boys dressed exactly alike for their performances. Their earliest outfits came straight from their closets: blue jeans, sneakers, white T-shirts, with unbuttoned denim jackets. They all had crew cuts and sunglasses.

The Hanson Brothers performed wherever they could. They sang at family reunions, office parties, and backyard barbecues. Many times they worked for free. However, soon the crowds were bigger and so was the money. People were amazed at these three young brothers.

In May 1992, the Hanson Brothers played at Mayfest. Mayfest is a popular musical festival in Tulsa. The boys performed brilliantly.

They were on stage for over an hour, doing a 15 song set. Of the 15 songs, they wrote six of them themselves.

The Hanson Brother's hobby was slowly developing into a dream to record their own music and be signed by a major record label. Ike, Tay, and Zac wanted music to be their life. They wanted to play in front of huge crowds. Their parents stood behind them, but also cautioned them to continue other hobbies, play sports, and study hard.

Isaac, Taylor, and Zac perform on the street outside the New York studio for NBC's "Today Show," May 12, 1997.

Taking Aim

The Hanson Brothers were trying to make it big and get a recording **contract**. They started singing with music in the background. When possible, one of them would play the piano.

The boys ditched their matching outfits and haircuts and just played it natural. The main thing they did was take their act on the road. The boys piled in the family van and performed all over the Midwest.

Because the brothers were home-schooled, they never missed a class. Their mother, Diana, was always with them. Before anything, they had to go to school and do their homework. Diana and Walker's support was more than just driving the boys around and being their teachers. They also were the boys' **managers**. Mom and dad did all of the legal work and made the calls and did the bookings.

The Hanson Brothers played everywhere from the Oklahoma State Fair to Branson, Missouri, to New Orleans, Louisiana. Of course, they still played in Tulsa, too. As the boys grew and worked harder, their music got better.

Everywhere the Hanson Brothers played, **audiences** responded enthusiastically. Ike, Tay, and Zac became more determined than ever to really make music their life. To make the dream come true, the Hanson family decided to treat the boys' music as more of a business than a hobby.

Making music became Hanson's goal.

Boomerang

Every time the Hanson Brothers played, more **fans** would show up. The fans liked the boys' music so much that they would always ask where they could buy a Hanson Brothers **album**. The Hanson Brothers didn't have an album out, however. Ike, Tay, and Zac decided it was time to record an album so their fans could play their music at home.

It took some time, but after a few months, the Hanson Brothers were ready to record. They sang along with hired studio musicians. Two **producers** came in to direct and mix the album. The result was the Hanson Brothers 1995 demo album *Boomerang*.

Although the album received no air play on the radio, it served its purpose. *Boomerang* sold many copies wherever the boys played. They sent the new album to every record company in the country—both big and small. All they got in return, however, were **rejections**.

Ike, Tay, and Zac were disappointed that no record company wanted them, but they didn't give up. In fact, they worked even harder and decided to take a different musical direction. They decided to make their own music, to not only sing but also play.

Since Tay was the best on the piano, he began playing the keyboards. Ike followed in his father's footsteps and began playing the guitar. A friend of the family gave Zac an old set of drums and that is how he got his instrument.

Within a month of learning their new instruments, the Hanson's were on the road playing. In the beginning, they did not sound that good. But the self-taught musicians kept working until they improved.

Hanson produced a demo album entitled Boomerang.

Another Album

In May of 1996, the Hanson Brothers released their second **album**. It was titled *MMMBop*. The song Hanson became famous for in the spring of 1997 was not a new song—in fact it wasn't even supposed to be a song!

The song "MMMBop" was meant to be a background part for another song written for the album *Boomerang*. But as time went on, the song got a life of its own. The Hanson Brothers again sold the records at their concerts. They also sent the new album out to many record companies.

This time the results were very different. Record companies loved this album. They liked the sound of the brothers, the way they played their own instruments, and that they wrote their own songs.

The record company Mercury offered the Hanson Brothers a **contract** in June of 1996. Little did Ike, Tay, and Zac know that from the moment they signed their contract, their lives would change forever.

The band changed its name to Hanson. They left for Los Angeles to record an all-new **album** for Mercury. Mercury hired the **producers** the Dust Brothers to help Hanson with the album. The entire Hanson family spent five months in Los Angeles recording the smash album *Middle of Nowhere*.

Taylor Hanson plays the bongo drums on stage at the 40th Annual Grammy Awards.

The Real Deal

When the **album** *Middle of Nowhere* was completed, everyone was excited. Ike, Tay, and Zac cowrote, sang, and played their instruments on every song on the album. The Dust Brothers produced many albums, including Beck's *Odelay*, but couldn't believe the talent these three young brothers had.

After critics heard the album, they were amazed at the boys' talent. Ike, Tay, and Zac were the real deal and had worked hard to get where they were. "MMMBop" was the first single from the album. The fun, upbeat song was an instant hit.

The song was being played on the radio throughout the country. The video for "MMMBop" was the number one requested video for many months. Hanson was very excited about their hit song, but they also stayed levelheaded. They knew how much work it had taken to succeed.

Hanson takes home another award.

The Sky's the Limit

Hanson has become one of the biggest names in the music business. They have been on award shows, MTV, VH1, *The Late Show, The Tonight Show,* and *Regis and Kathie Lee,* to name a few.

Hanson is famous around the world. Their **fans** love them. Young girls adore them, adults can be seen tapping their feet or singing along with their songs, and critics respect and admire their work.

The best part about Hanson is that they worked hard and stayed grounded. They love going back to their hometown and hanging out with their family and friends. They have never forgotten what it took to succeed. The Hanson boys made music because they loved it, not for the fame or money.

The future is bright for the multi-talented brothers from the middle of nowhere. After devoting most of their life to music, they now have become three of the most famous people in the music industry. With the talent, devotion, and work ethic the brothers possess, the sky's the limit.

Hanson backstage after winning an MTV Award.

Secrets about Hanson

•Ike, Tay, and Zac carry journals around with them wherever they go. They write down new song ideas and cool adventures they have on the road.

•When "MMMBop" hit number one, it made music trivia history. They are the second group comprised of just three brothers who hit number one. The other was the Bee Gees.

•"MMMBop" also made history by reaching number one in the United States and England at the same time. It is the first debut song by any group in history to do that.

•The first time Hanson heard "MMMBop" on the radio, they were just getting out of a van, hurrying to an interview. They all jumped back in the van and cranked up the radio. They all remember it being a very awesome and weird feeling.

The Final Words From Hanson

Ike's point of view: "Music is a part of us. It's what we've always done and intend to be doing for a long time. Music is our life. It's what we love."

Tay's thoughts: "I hope we stay in the music business. But we also want to pursue the whole entertainment industry, because we're interested in doing movies."

Zac sums it up: "We will be doing something together forever. We can never breakup. We're brothers!"

Glossary

A Cappella: an Italian word that means singing without any instruments in the background.

Accountant: a person who keeps track of an individual's or a business' financial records.

Album: a set of songs that is put together by a musical group. An album can come in different forms including CD or tape.

Audience: a group of people who watch a performance.

Composing: the act of writing the music or lyrics to a song.

Contract: a legal document that a person or group signs that says they will record a certain number of albums and how much they will be paid.

Cultural: the beliefs or values of certain groups or countries.

Fans: people who support a musical group by attending their concerts, buying their albums, and listening to their music.

Harmonize: the combination of different voices and different tones.

Lyrics: the words in a song.

Manager: a person who is in charge of taking care of the daily business of a musical group, such as scheduling concerts, working on contracts, etc.

Producer: a person who puts the album together after the recording of the music has been completed.

Rejections: being turned down for something you are trying to accomplish.

Hanson on the Web

E-Mail Hanson:

hansonfans@hansonline.com

www.hansonline.com is the band's official site. It features sounds and photos not available anywhere else. It is updated with new information on the band almost every week.

www.hansonhitz.com This is one of the best Hanson sites around. It features photos, articles, interviews, lyrics, chat rooms, and much more.

Pass It On

Tell readers around the country information you've learned about your favorite superstars. Share your little-known facts and interesting stories.
We want to hear from you!
To get posted on the ABDO Publishing Company Web site, E-mail us at "Adventure@abdopub.com"
Download a free screen saver at www.abdopub.com

Index

A

Aerosmith 7
album 8, 11, 20, 22, 23, 24

B

Bee Gees 28
bookings 18
Boomerang 20, 22

C

Canada 4
church 8
composing 10
Counting Crows 7
country and western 8
critics 24, 26

D

drums 7, 21
Dust Brothers 23, 24

E

England 4, 28

F

fans 20, 26

G

guitar 8, 21

H

Hanson Brothers 16, 18, 19, 20, 22
harmonize 5, 10
homework 18
Horizons 8

I

in-line skating 6, 7, 10
instruments 5, 15, 21, 22, 24

L

Late Show, The 26
Los Angeles 23
lyrics 5, 14

M

manager 18
Mayfest 16
Mercury Records 4
Middle of Nowhere 8, 23, 24
"MMMBop" 4, 5, 22, 24, 28
Morissette, Alanis 6
MTV 26

O

Oklahoma State Fair 19

P

parents 8, 10, 13, 14, 17
piano 14, 16, 18, 21
producers 20, 23

R

"Rain Falling Down." 14
Regis and Kathie Lee 26
rock-n-roll 10, 15

S

school 12, 18
sister 14
songs 10, 15, 16, 17, 22, 26
sports 6, 7, 10, 17
studio 20

T

Tonight Show, The 26
Tulsa, Oklahoma 4, 8

U

United States 4, 13, 28

V

VH1 26
video 5, 10, 24